Trump Articles of Impeachment

25 Grounds for Removal

by RootsAction.org

Trump Articles of Impeachment

Book design by David Swanson.

Cover photo by Gage Skidmore.

Printed in the USA

First Edition / November 2019

ISBN: 978-0-9980859-9-9

CONTENTS

INTRODUCTION

RootsAction.org is one of the two organizations that launched the Impeach Donald Trump Now petition on Inauguration Day in January 2017, based on the first two of the following 25 grounds for impeachment. That petition has gathered 1.4 million signers.

Since then, RootsAction has developed the other 23 articles of impeachment published below, and flooded Congress Members with hundreds of thousands of emails from their constituents urging that these or similar articles be introduced and voted on. We encourage readers to give this book to Congress Members and let them know that you want at least some of these articles of impeachment introduced, passed, and sent to the Senate for a trial.

Following the articles of impeachment in this book is an outline of an impeachment strategy, followed by a list of frequently asked questions together with answers from RootsAction.

1. *Violation of Constitution on Domestic Emoluments*

In his conduct while President of the United States, Donald J. Trump, in violation of his constitutional oath to faithfully execute the office of President of the United States and, to the best of his ability, preserve, protect, and defend the Constitution of the United States, and in violation of his constitutional duty under Article II, Section 1 of the Constitution "to take care that the laws be faithfully executed," has illegally received emoluments from the United States government and from individual state governments.

The Constitutional ban on domestic emoluments (Article II, Section 1) is absolute, not waivable by Congress, and not subject to proving any particular corrupting influence.

President Trump's lease of the Old Post Office Building in Washington D.C. violates the General Services Administration lease contract which states: "No … elected official of the Government of the United States … shall be admitted to any share or part of this Lease, or to any benefit that may arise therefrom." The GSA's failure to enforce that contract constitutes an emolument. A January 16, 2019, report by the Inspector General of the General Services Administration confirmed this.

Since 1980 Trump and his businesses have garnered, according to the *New York Times*, "$885 million in tax breaks, grants and other subsidies for luxury apartments, hotels and office buildings in New York." Those subsidies from the state of New York have continued since President Trump took office and constitute emoluments. The Trump organization receives emoluments from other states as well.

In these and many similar actions and decisions, President Donald J. Trump has acted in a manner contrary to his trust as President, and subversive of constitutional government, to the prejudice of the cause of law and justice and to the manifest injury of the people of the United States. Wherefore, President

Donald J. Trump, by such conduct, is guilty of an impeachable offense warranting removal from office.

2. Violation of Constitution on Foreign Emoluments

In his conduct while President of the United States, Donald J. Trump, in violation of his constitutional oath to faithfully execute the office of President of the United States and, to the best of his ability, preserve, protect, and defend the Constitution of the United States, and in violation of his constitutional duty under Article II, Section 1 of the Constitution "to take care that the laws be faithfully executed," has illegally received emoluments from foreign governments. Foreign emoluments are banned by the U.S. Constitution (Article I, Section 9).

Donald J. Trump's business has licensing deals with two Trump Towers in Istanbul, Turkey. Donald J. Trump has stated: "I have a little conflict of interest, because I have a major, major building in Istanbul."

China's state-owned Industrial and Commercial Bank of China is the largest tenant in Trump Tower in New York City. It is also a major lender to the Trump organization. Its rent payments and its loans put President Trump in violation of the U.S. Constitution.

Foreign diplomats, including the Embassy of Kuwait, have changed their Washington D.C. hotel and event reservations to Trump International Hotel following Donald J. Trump's election to public office.

In these and many similar actions and decisions, President Donald J. Trump has acted in a manner contrary to his trust as President, and subversive of constitutional government, to the prejudice of the cause of law and justice and to the manifest injury of the people of the United States. Wherefore, President Donald J. Trump, by such conduct, is guilty of an impeachable offense warranting removal from office.

3. *Incitement of Violence*

In his conduct while President of the United States, and while campaigning for election to that office, Donald J. Trump, in violation of his constitutional oath to faithfully execute the office of President of the United States and, to the best of his ability, preserve, protect, and defend the Constitution of the United States, and in violation of his constitutional duty under Article II, Section 1 of the Constitution "to take care that the laws be faithfully executed," has illegally incited violence within the United States.

A partial sampling of public statements by candidate Donald J. Trump:

"If you see somebody getting ready to throw a tomato, knock the crap out of them. I promise you, I will pay for the legal fees."

"You know what I hate? There's a guy, totally disruptive, throwing punches, we're not allowed to punch back anymore. I love the old days—you know what they used to do to guys like that when they were in a place like this? They'd be carried out on a stretcher, folks."

"See the first group, I was nice. Oh, take your time. The second group, I was pretty nice. The third group, I'll be a little more violent. And the fourth group, I'll say get the hell out of here!"

"I'd like to punch him in the face, I tell ya."

"He was swinging, he was hitting people, and the audience hit back. That's what we need more of."

Numerous incidents of violence followed these and other similar comments. John Franklin McGraw punched a man in the face at a Trump event, and then told *Inside Edition* that "The next time we see him, we might have to kill him." Donald J. Trump said that he was considering paying McGraw's legal bills.

Since Trump's election and inauguration, his

comments appearing to incite violence have continued, as have incidents of violence in which those participating in violence have pointed to Trump as justification.

On July 2, 2017, President Donald J. Trump tweeted a video of himself body slamming a man with an image of "CNN" superimposed on him.

In August 2017, participants in a racist rally in Charlottesville, Va., credited President Trump with boosting their cause. Their violence included actions that led to a murder charge. President Trump publicly minimized the offense and sought to blame "many sides."

In April 2019, weeks after one of his supporters was arrested by the FBI for threatening to shoot Congresswoman Ilhan Omar in the head, President Trump tweeted a misleading and inflammatory video promoting just the sort of hatred toward Omar that the man arrested had expressed.

In these and similar actions and decisions, President Donald J. Trump has acted in a manner contrary to his trust as President, and subversive of constitutional government, to the prejudice of the cause of law and justice and to the manifest injury of the people of the United States. Wherefore, President Donald J. Trump, by such conduct, is guilty of an impeachable offense warranting removal from office.

4. Interference With Voting Rights

In his conduct while President of the United States, and while campaigning for election to that office, Donald J. Trump, in violation of his constitutional oath to faithfully execute the office of President of the United States and, to the best of his ability, preserve, protect, and defend the Constitution of the United States, and in violation of his constitutional duty under Article II, Section 1 of the Constitution "to take care that the laws be faithfully executed," has engaged in acts of voter intimidation and suppression.

For months leading up to the November 2016 elections, Donald J. Trump publicly encouraged his supporters, the same ones he had encouraged to engage in violence, to patrol polling places in search of participants in the virtually nonexistent practice of voter fraud. In so doing, candidate Trump made would-be voters aware that they might face such patrols. His remarks included:

"I hope you people can sort of not just vote on the 8th, go around and look and watch other polling places, and make sure that it's 100 percent fine."

"We're going to watch Pennsylvania. Go down to certain areas and watch and study and make sure other people don't come in and vote five times."

Trump urged supporters to target Philadelphia, St. Louis, and other cities with large minority populations.

He created on his campaign website a way to sign up to "volunteer to be a Trump election observer."

When early voting began, incidents were reported of Trump supporters photographing voters and otherwise intimidating them.

Trump ally and advisor Roger Stone formed an activist group called Stop the Steal that acted in line with Trump's public statements. The group appeared to threaten violence against delegates if the Republican Party denied Trump its nomination. It then organized intimidation efforts in the general election around the unsupported claim that Trump's opponents would somehow "flood the polls with illegals. Liberal enclaves already let illegals vote in their local and state elections and now they want them to vote in the Presidential election."

According to the U.S. Department of Justice in 2006, in all federal elections from 2002 to 2005, a total of 26 people out of 197 million were convicted of trying to vote illegally.

Stone's organization created official-looking ID badges for volunteers and asked them to videotape voters, and conduct phony exit polls in nine cities with large minority populations.

One such volunteer, Steve Webb of Ohio, told the *Boston Globe*, "I'm going to go right up behind them. I'll do everything legally. I want to see if they are accountable. I'm not going to do anything illegal. I'm going to make them a little bit nervous."

Since becoming president, Donald J. Trump has continued with voter intimidation efforts. He has created a Presidential Advisory Commission on Election Integrity, which has sent letters to states requesting sensitive voter information. Most states have refused. But thousands of people have canceled their registrations rather than have their information turned over to Trump's administration.

In these and similar actions and decisions, President Donald J. Trump has acted in a manner contrary to his trust as President, and subversive of constitutional government, to the prejudice of the cause of law and justice and to the manifest injury of the people of the United States. Wherefore, President Donald J. Trump, by such conduct, is guilty of an impeachable offense warranting removal from office.

5. Discrimination Based On Religion

In his conduct while President of the United States, Donald J. Trump, in violation of his constitutional oath to faithfully execute the office of President of the United States and, to the best of his ability, preserve, protect, and defend the Constitution of the United States, and in violation of his constitutional duty under Article II, Section 1 of the Constitution "to take care that the laws be faithfully executed," has engaged in acts of discrimination in violation of the First Amendment and other laws by seeking to ban Muslims from entering the United States.

Donald J. Trump had openly campaigned for office promising a "total and complete shutdown of Muslims entering the United States." Once in office, he created an executive order that his advisor Rudy Giuliani, said on Fox News had been drafted after Trump had asked him for the best way to create a Muslim ban "legally." The order targeted several majority-Muslim countries for restrictions on immigration to the United States, but made allowances for people of minority religions within those countries. Trump told the Christian Broadcasting Network that Christian refugees would be given priority. When a federal court stopped this order from taking effect, President Trump issued a new one containing, in the words of his advisor Stephen Miller "minor technical differences."

In these actions and decisions, President Donald J. Trump has acted in a manner contrary to his trust as President, and subversive of constitutional government, to the prejudice of the cause of law and justice and to the manifest injury of the people of the United States. Wherefore, President Donald J. Trump, by such conduct, is guilty of an impeachable offense warranting removal from office.

6. *Illegal War*

In his conduct while President of the United States, Donald J. Trump, in violation of his constitutional oath to faithfully execute the office of President of the United States and, to the best of his ability, preserve, protect, and defend the Constitution of the United States, and in violation of his constitutional duty under Article II, Section 1 of the Constitution "to take care that the laws be faithfully executed," has waged numerous wars in violation of the United Nations Charter and of the Kellogg-Briand Pact, both treaties part of the Supreme Law of the United States under Article VI of the U.S. Constitution.

President Trump and his subordinates attempted to mislead the U.S. public and Congress about justifications for wars, including by claiming to have knowledge that the Syrian government used chemical weapons, as well as by falsely stating the number of U.S. troops deployed to various wars.

President Trump has escalated bombing campaigns in Iraq and Syria, resulting in large numbers of civilian deaths. After campaigning for office in opposition to the war on Afghanistan, Trump has effectively made it a permanent operation. President Trump spoke at the headquarters of the Central Intelligence Agency on January 23, 2017, and promoted an illegal policy of waging wars for the theft of resources. Trump has overseen the U.S. military's collaboration in the illegal bombing of Yemen by Saudi Arabia, in violation of the Leahy Law and resulting in a severe humanitarian crisis.

By these actions, President Donald J. Trump has acted in a manner contrary to his trust as President, and subversive of constitutional government, to the prejudice of the cause of law and justice and to the manifest injury of the people of the United States and the world. Wherefore, President Donald J. Trump, by such conduct, is guilty of an impeachable offense warranting removal from office.

7. Illegal Threat of Nuclear War

In his conduct while President of the United States, Donald J. Trump, in violation of his constitutional oath to faithfully execute the office of President of the United States and, to the best of his ability, preserve, protect, and defend the Constitution of the United States, and in violation of his constitutional duty under Article II, Section 1 of the Constitution "to take care that the laws be faithfully executed," has flagrantly threatened nuclear war ("fire and fury") against North Korea, in violation of the United Nations Charter, a treaty that is part of the Supreme Law of the United States under Article VI of the U.S. Constitution.

Trump later threatened Iran with "CONSEQUENCES THE LIKES OF WHICH FEW THROUGHOUT HISTORY HAVE EVER SUFFERED BEFORE," also declaring "If Iran wants to fight, that will be the official end of Iran."

By these and similar actions, President Donald J. Trump has acted in a manner contrary to his trust as President, and subversive of constitutional government, to the prejudice of the cause of law and justice and to the manifest injury of the people of the United States and the world. Wherefore, President Donald J. Trump, by such conduct, is guilty of an impeachable offense warranting removal from office.

8. Abuse of Pardon Power

In his conduct while President of the United States, Donald J. Trump, in violation of his constitutional oath to faithfully execute the office of President of the United States and, to the best of his ability, preserve, protect, and defend the Constitution of the United States, and in violation of his constitutional duty under Article II, Section 1 of the Constitution "to take care that the laws be faithfully executed," has issued a pardon for former sheriff of Maricopa County, Arizona, Joe Arpaio, who had been convicted of contempt for failure to comply with a court order in a case charging him with racial discrimination.

Arpaio was open about his commission of the underlying crime, for which he was found liable in a civil suit. His contempt conviction was for continuing to engage in racial profiling, violating an order to cease doing so.

Arpaio set up a prison that he called a concentration camp. It had a high death rate with deaths often unexplained. He enclosed Latino prisoners with electric fencing.

According to *Washington Post* reporting, Trump has directed his subordinates to illegally seize private land and violate environmental regulations in order to build a wall on the Mexican border, and has promised to pardon all the crimes involved.

By this action, President Donald J. Trump has acted in a manner contrary to his trust as President, and subversive of constitutional government, to the prejudice of the cause of law and justice and to the manifest injury of the people of the United States and the world. Wherefore, President Donald J. Trump, by such conduct, is guilty of an impeachable offense warranting removal from office.

9. Obstruction of Justice

In his conduct while President of the United States, Donald J. Trump, in violation of his constitutional oath to faithfully execute the office of President of the United States and, to the best of his ability, preserve, protect, and defend the Constitution of the United States, and in violation of his constitutional duty under Article II, Section 1 of the Constitution "to take care that the laws be faithfully executed," has obstructed justice.

The day after President Trump was briefed by White House Counsel on dishonest statements by then-National Security Advisor Michael Flynn who was being investigated by the FBI, Trump met with the director of the FBI James Comey and demanded his personal loyalty. Two weeks later Trump asked Comey to drop the investigation. Later still, Trump fired Comey. By Trump's own words (nbcnews. to/2s0iLJq), his motivation was at least partly to obstruct the investigation.

By this action, President Donald J. Trump has acted in a manner contrary to his trust as President, and subversive of constitutional government, to the prejudice of the cause of law and justice and to the manifest injury of the people of the United States and the world. Wherefore, President Donald J. Trump, by such conduct, is guilty of an impeachable offense warranting removal from office.

10. Politicizing Prosecutions

In his conduct while President of the United States, Donald J. Trump, in violation of his constitutional oath to faithfully execute the office of President of the United States and, to the best of his ability, preserve, protect, and defend the Constitution of the

United States, and in violation of his constitutional duty under Article II, Section 1 of the Constitution "to take care that the laws be faithfully executed," has directed or endeavored to direct law enforcement, including the Department of Justice and the Federal Bureau of Investigation, to investigate and prosecute political adversaries and others -- and to not prosecute political allies -- for improper purposes not justified by any lawful function of his office, thereby eroding the rule of law, undermining the independence of law enforcement from politics, and compromising the constitutional right to due process of law.

On the Friday before Election Day 2017, the president issued a remarkable series of public statements, including on Twitter, pressuring the U.S. Department of Justice to investigate Hillary Clinton, the Democratic Party, and other political adversaries.

Earlier, the president had called Army soldier Bowe Bergdahl a "dirty, rotten traitor" while court-martial charges were pending.

On September 3, 2018, President Donald J. Trump tweeted this: "Two long running, Obama era, investigations of two very popular Republican Congressmen were brought to a well publicized charge, just ahead of the Mid-Terms, by the Jeff Sessions Justice Department. Two easy wins now in doubt because there is not enough time. Good job Jeff…" This cannot be read but as potentially influencing the current or a future Attorney General or others in law enforcement to politicize prosecutions.

In 1940, Attorney General (later Supreme Court Justice) Robert Jackson warned that "the greatest danger of abuse of prosecuting power" was "picking the man and then . . . putting investigators to work, to pin some offense on him." A chief executive who uses law enforcement to persecute political enemies is characteristic of a banana republic, not a constitutional republic. That is why Republican and Democratic presidents alike have respected the independence of law enforcement. In the case of military courts-martial, such as Bergdahl's, this limit is formalized in the prohibition of "command influence."

Congress set a precedent with the second article of impeachment against President Richard Nixon, which cited, in its fifth specification, his use of federal investigative agencies against political opponents. Following this precedent, the president's attempts to employ the criminal investigative powers of the federal government against political opponents "for purposes unrelated to national security, the enforcement of laws, or any other lawful function of his office" are grounds for impeachment, even if they did not succeed in influencing law enforcement.

By this action, President Donald J. Trump has acted in a manner contrary to his trust as President, and subversive of constitutional government, to the prejudice of the cause of law and justice and to the manifest injury of the people of the United States and the world. Wherefore, President Donald J. Trump, by such conduct, is guilty of an impeachable offense warranting removal from office.

11. Collusion Against the United States with a Foreign Government

In his conduct while President-Elect of the United States, Donald J. Trump and his transition team lobbied foreign governments, including those of Egypt and Russia on behalf of the government of Israel.

Trump advisor Michael Flynn has lied to the Federal Bureau of Investigation about talking, pre-inauguration, to Russia (and other countries) on behalf of the government of Israel, allegedly at the instruction of Jared Kushner, who reportedly took his direction from Israeli Prime Minister Benjamin Netanyahu.

Prime Minister Netanyahu wanted Russia to block or delay a UN resolution against illegal Israeli settlements, because then-President of the United States Barack Obama had chosen not to veto it. News reports in December 2016 said that Russia, while it did not veto, did try to delay the vote. Also, in December 2016, the government of Egypt said it had delayed the vote because President-Elect Trump had phoned the president of Egypt on behalf of Israel.

In these actions and decisions, Donald J. Trump has acted in a manner subversive of constitutional government, to the prejudice of the cause of law and justice and to the manifest injury of the people of the United States. Wherefore, President Donald J. Trump, by such conduct, is guilty of an impeachable offense warranting removal from office.

12. Failure to Reasonably Prepare for or Respond to Hurricanes Harvey and Maria

In his conduct while President of the United States, Donald J. Trump, in violation of his constitutional oath to faithfully execute the office of President of the United States and, to the best of his ability, preserve, protect, and defend the Constitution of the United States, which was established to "provide for the common defense," and in violation of his constitutional duty under Article II, Section 1 of the Constitution "to take care that the laws be faithfully executed," has failed to reasonably prepare for events like Hurricane Harvey and Hurricane Maria or to adequately respond to those hurricanes.

The Federal Emergency Management Agency (FEMA) was without a new director until June 2017. The National Hurricane Center was without a head from May 2017 through the time of Hurricane Harvey in August. On August 15, 2017, President Trump issued an executive order that rejected the Federal Flood Risk Management Standard, which had been established by executive order in 2015, and which required that infrastructure be built to withstand flooding. He already had disbanded the Advisory Committee for the Sustained National Climate Assessment, and withdrawn the United States from the Paris climate agreement. When Hurricane Harvey hit, President Donald Trump did not engage in rescue and recovery operations on the scale required. His subordinates at FEMA proposed that private individuals fund and perform those tasks on their own.

When Hurricane Maria hit Puerto Rico in September 2017, and for the months that followed, President Trump refused significant aid, despite widespread devastation, lack of electricity, and lack of medical care that, according to a study published in the *New England Journal of Medicine* in May 2018, left over 4,600 people dead. For weeks Trump even blocked aid to Puerto Rico from other nations, refusing to waive the Jones Act as he had done following Hurricane Harvey, even as numerous experts predicted the sort of death and suffering that resulted.

By these actions, President Donald J. Trump has acted in a manner contrary to his trust as President, and subversive of constitutional government, to the prejudice of the cause of law and justice and to the manifest injury of the people of the United States and the world. Wherefore, President Donald J.

Trump, by such conduct, is guilty of an impeachable offense warranting removal from office.

13. Separating Children and Infants from Families

In his conduct while President of the United States, Donald J. Trump, in violation of his constitutional oath to faithfully execute the office of President of the United States and, to the best of his ability, preserve, protect, and defend the Constitution of the United States, and in violation of his constitutional duty under Article II, Section 1 of the Constitution "to take care that the laws be faithfully executed," has overseen the work of his subordinates who have forcibly separated thousands of refugee children and infants from their families, imprisoned them in inhumane conditions including on military bases and in the private facilities of military contractors, denied access to these sites sought by members of Congress, failed to meet or even to plausibly attempt to meet a court-imposed deadline to reunite children with their families, and defended these policies with hate-inspiring rhetoric almost certainly resulting in additional violence and cruelty by government employees and private individuals alike (see also Article of Impeachment on "Incitement of Violence").

In these actions, Donald J. Trump has abused his high office and violated numerous legal requirements in an explicit effort to punish and deter people who in many cases stand accused of no legal violations themselves, and in other cases are accused of a misdemeanor. These actions by President Trump have violated the Universal Declaration of Human Rights to which the United States is party, the Convention on the Rights of the Child to which every other nation on earth is party, the Eighth Amendment to the U.S. Constitution, and the Due Process clause of the Fifth Amendment to the U.S. Constitution. The U.S. Supreme Court has maintained that "the interest of parents in the care, custody, and control of their children is perhaps the oldest of the fundamental liberty interests recognized by [the] Court." President

Trump's subsequent Executive Order stating that families would be imprisoned as groups, rather than being separated, would have failed to bring him into compliance with international law or the Constitution even if implemented.

On September 6, 2018, the Trump administration announced a new rule that would allow immigrant children with their parents to be imprisoned indefinitely, in violation of a 1997 court settlement agreement that limits the imprisonment of children to 20 days.

In these actions and decisions, President Donald J. Trump has acted in a manner contrary to his trust as President, and subversive of constitutional government, to the prejudice of the cause of law and justice and to the manifest injury of the people of the United States and people seeking asylum and refuge in the United States. Wherefore, President Donald J. Trump, by such conduct, is guilty of an impeachable offense warranting removal from office.

14. Illegally Attempting to Influence an Election

While campaigning for the office of President of the United States, Donald J. Trump, according to the sworn testimony and the guilty plea of his attorney Michael Cohen, engaged in a criminal conspiracy to buy the silence of individuals, and did so with the intent of influencing the election and in violation of campaign finance laws.

On August 21, 2018, Cohen admitted in federal court that he had paid Stormy Daniels and Karen McDougal to silence them before the 2016 election at Donald J. Trump's "direction." Cohen said he acted "in coordination with and at the direction of a candidate for federal office" and "for the principal purpose of influencing the election." This testimony implicates Donald J. Trump in the crime of conspiring to make an excessive and illegal campaign contribution. It also implicates him in the high crime and misdemeanor of attempting to fraudulently influence -- and quite possibly successfully influence -- the outcome of a

U.S. presidential election. As President, he lied about and tried to cover-up his wrongdoing.

In this action, President Donald J. Trump has acted in a manner contrary to his trust as President, and subversive of constitutional government, to the prejudice of the cause of law and justice and to the manifest injury of the people of the United States. Wherefore, President Donald J. Trump, by such conduct, is guilty of an impeachable offense warranting removal from office.

15 Tax Fraud and Public Misrepresentation

In his conduct prior to assuming the office of President of the United States, Donald J. Trump engaged in extensive tax fraud which served as the basis for his dramatic misrepresentation to the public of his accomplishments.

According to evidence and documentation made

public by the *New York Times* and not countered by President Trump, he and his siblings committed numerous felonies in the course of obtaining wealth from their father while paying approximately 5% rather than the 55% in taxes that the law required.

They did this, in part, by undervaluing properties, a crime known as appraisal fraud. Donald Trump and his siblings claimed that properties given them by their father were worth $41.4 million, but sold those properties for over 16 times that amount during the next decade.

Another crime employed was transfer pricing. Trump and his siblings massively overcharged their father's companies for largely nonexistent services in order to both obtain his wealth and reduce his profits. The reduction in profits allowed Trump's father to increase the rent he charged people for publicly subsidized, rent-controlled properties.

Through these and other fraudulent activities, Donald Trump was made wealthy by the transfer of money from his father. In the analysis of one expert, if Trump had simply invested that money in a simple investment fund, he would now have the $10 billion he falsely claimed to have as a candidate for president. In reality, Trump lost a fortune through business failures. As a candidate, however, by lying about his wealth and the origins of his wealth, Donald Trump misled voters to believe that, while he had no political record he did have a very successful business record. Trump falsely claimed to have received only $1 million from his father which he had been required to pay back "with interest."

In these and many similar actions and decisions, President Donald J. Trump has acted in a manner contrary to his trust as President, and subversive of constitutional government, to the prejudice of the cause of law and justice and to the manifest injury of the people of the United States. Wherefore, President Donald J. Trump, by such conduct, is guilty of an impeachable offense warranting removal from office.

16. Assaulting Freedom of the Press

In his conduct while President of the United States, Donald J. Trump, in violation of his constitutional oath to faithfully execute the office of President of the United States and, to the best of his ability, preserve, protect, and defend the Constitution of the United States, and in violation of his constitutional duty under Article II, Section 1 of the Constitution "to take care that the laws be faithfully executed," has repeatedly undermined the freedom of the press.

President Trump has threatened to use libel law to go after media outlets that have displeased him. On March 30, 2017, he tweeted: "The failing @nytimes has disgraced the media world. Gotten me wrong for two solid years. Change libel laws?" On April 30, 2017, his then chief of staff Reince Priebus confirmed that changing libel laws is "something we've looked at," adding that "newspapers and news agencies need to be more responsible with how they report the news." On July 2, 2017, President Donald

J. Trump tweeted a video of himself body slamming a man with an image of "CNN" superimposed on him.

President Trump has threatened to remove broadcasting licenses from media outlets that have displeased him. On October 11, 2017, he tweeted: "With all of the Fake News coming out of NBC and the Networks at what point is it appropriate to challenge their License? Bad for country!" and "Network news has become so partisan, distorted and fake that licenses must be challenged and, if appropriate, revoked. Not fair to public!"

President Trump's White House, on February 24, 2017, barred certain news media — CNN, the *New York Times*, the *L.A. Times*, and *Politico* — from attending a White House press briefing. In June 2017, his administration prohibited video recordings of White House press briefings. In November 2018, his administration suspended the press credential of CNN correspondent Jim Acosta, falsely accusing him of "placing his hands" on a white house intern.

President Trump has repeatedly referred to news media as "the enemy of the people," while expressing his desire that journalistic activity be stifled. For example: On February 17, 2017, Trump tweeted: "The FAKE NEWS media (failing @nytimes, @ NBCNews, @ABC, @CBS, @CNN) is not my enemy, it is the enemy of the American People!". On July 22, 2017, Trump tweeted: "A new INTELLIGENCE LEAK from the Amazon Washington Post, this time against A.G. Jeff Sessions. These illegal leaks, like Comey's, must stop!"

President Trump's rhetoric has encouraged authoritarian foreign governments to attack the very U.S. media that Trump criticizes, endangering not only press freedoms but the lives and safety of American journalists. On May 2, 2017, just ahead of World Press Freedom Day, the Committee to Protect Journalists noted that "President Trump's oft-tweeted 'fake news' epithet, for example, had already been adopted by repressive governments such as China, Syria, and Russia. When Trump verbally attacked a correspondent during a February press conference, he was cheered by Turkey President Recep Tayyip Erdoğan, the world's worst jailer of journalists.

When Saudi Arabia murdered U.S./Saudi journalist Jamal Khashoggi, President Trump made extensive efforts to deny the evidence and to prevent or minimize the consequences to the Saudi government, even while continuing his usual verbal attacks on U.S. journalists.

President Trump's subordinates locked up U.S./Iranian journalist Marzieh Hashemi with no charges or trial as a "material witness."

President Trump's Department of Justice has indicted Australian publisher Julian Assange on espionage charges for Wikileaks' acts of journalism and publishing.

President Trump appointed William Barr as U.S. Attorney General; Barr stated at his confirmation hearings that he might jail journalists for doing their job if that job "hurt the country."

Freedom of the press is enshrined in the First Amendment to the U.S. Constitution. As Justice Black observed in *New York Times Co. v. United States*, "In the First Amendment the Founding Fathers gave the free press the protection it must have to fulfill its essential role in our democracy. The press was to serve the governed, not the governors. The Government's power to censor the press was abolished so that the press would remain forever free to censure the Government. The press was protected so that it could bare the secrets of government and inform the people. Only a free and unrestrained press can effectively expose deception in government."

A president is certainly free to criticize particular news stories and outlets that he believes are inaccurate — and no above-cited tweet or statement, standing in isolation, would constitute an impeachable offense. However, President Trump's consistent pattern of verbal attacks against journalists and his administration's actions to retaliate against and exclude journalists, combined with threats to take governmental action against news outlets, crosses a line.

In the above and many similar actions and decisions, President Donald J. Trump has acted in a manner contrary to his trust as President, and subversive of constitutional government, to the prejudice of the cause of law and justice and to the manifest injury of the people of the United States. Wherefore, President Donald J. Trump, by such conduct, is guilty of an impeachable offense warranting removal from office.

17. Supporting a Coup in Venezuela

In his conduct while President of the United States, Donald J. Trump, in violation of his constitutional oath to faithfully execute the office of President of the United States and, to the best of his ability, preserve, protect, and defend the Constitution of the United States, and in violation of his constitutional duty under Article II, Section 1 of the Constitution "to take care that the laws be faithfully executed,"

And in his conduct while Vice President of the United States, Michael Richard Pence, in violation of his oath to faithfully execute the office of Vice President of the United States and to support and defend the Constitution of the United States,

have damaged the rule of law and endangered international security by supporting a coup attempt in Venezuela.

On the evening of January 22, 2019, following years of damaging U.S. sanctions against Venezuela, which followed an unsuccessful 2002 U.S.-supported coup attempt, Vice President Pence reportedly called Juan Guaidó and told him that the United States would support him if he were to seize power in Venezuela. The next day, January 23, Guaidó attempted to do so. That same day, President Trump issued a statement recognizing Guaidó as the President of Venezuela, despite the fact that Venezuela had an elected president and that Guaidó had no legitimate claim to the presidency. On January 24, 2019, the Trump-Pence administration attempted unsuccessfully to persuade the Organization of American States to recognize Guaidó as president.

In the above and related actions and decisions, President Donald J. Trump and Vice President Michael Richard Pence have acted in a manner contrary to their trust as President and Vice President, and subversive of constitutional government, to the prejudice of the cause of law and justice and to the manifest injury of the people of the United States. Wherefore, President Donald J. Trump and Michael Richard Pence, by such conduct, are guilty of an impeachable offense warranting removal from office.

18. Unconstitutional Declaration of Emergency

In his conduct while President of the United States, Donald J. Trump, in violation of his constitutional oath to faithfully execute the office of President of the United States and, to the best of his ability, preserve, protect, and defend the Constitution of the United States, and in violation of his constitutional duty under Article II, Section 1 of the Constitution "to take care that the laws be faithfully executed," has declared a national emergency, in the absence of any actual emergency, for the purpose of spending money on a border wall that had been appropriated for other purposes.

In so acting, President Trump has violated Article 1, Section 7 of the United States Constitution: "All Bills for raising Revenue shall originate in the House of Representatives . . . ." He has also, in so acting, violated Article 1, Section 8 of the Constitution: "No Money shall be drawn from the Treasury, but in Consequence of Appropriations made by Law . . . ." The same action also violates the Federal Anti-Deficiency Statute. By using the United States military to enforce immigration law, President Trump's announced plan would also violate the Posse Comitatus Act.

In addition, President Trump has abused his power by publicly promoting this action using a series of falsehoods encouraging fear, bigotry, and hatred. He has falsely suggested that immigrants commit crimes at a higher rate than non-immigrants, that illegal border crossings have been increasing in recent years, that terrorist groups have sent operatives to enter the United States through Mexico, and that applying for asylum is a threatening or criminal action.

In these and many similar actions and decisions, President Donald J. Trump has acted in a manner contrary to his trust as President, and subversive of constitutional government, to the prejudice of the cause of law and justice and to the manifest injury of the people of the United States. Wherefore, President Donald J. Trump, by such conduct, is guilty of an impeachable offense warranting removal from office.

19. *Instructing Border Patrol to Violate the Law*

In his conduct while President of the United States, Donald J. Trump, in violation of his constitutional oath to faithfully execute the office of President of the United States and, to the best of his ability, preserve, protect, and defend the Constitution of the United States, and in violation of his constitutional duty under Article II, Section 1 of the Constitution "to take care that the laws be faithfully executed," has directed U.S. Border Patrol agents to violate the law.

On April 5, 2019, President Trump, while visiting Calexico, California, reportedly told Border Patrol agents to defy U.S. law and refuse to allow migrants into the United States. The President went further, instructing Border Patrol agents to lie to a judge if charged with violating the law. "If judges give you trouble, say, 'Sorry, judge, I can't do it. We don't have the room,'" said the President. Upon the President's departure, Border Patrol officials instructed their agents that, contrary to the President's instructions, they were required to obey the law.

President Trump went further still, informing Customs and Border Protection Commissioner Kevin McAleenan, according to "senior administration officials" who spoke with CNN, that he would "grant McAleenan a pardon if he were sent to jail for having border agents block asylum seekers from entering the U.S. in defiance of US law."

Paralleling his lawless efforts to keep refugees and immigrants out of the United States, President Trump continued to promote his policy of separating infants and children from families (see separate Article of Impeachment), and proposed shipping and releasing imprisoned refugees to particular parts of the United States for reasons of electoral politics, not human welfare.

In these and many similar actions and decisions, President Donald J. Trump has acted in a manner contrary to his trust as President, and subversive of constitutional government, to the prejudice of the cause of law and justice and to the manifest injury of the people of the United States. Wherefore, President Donald J. Trump, by such conduct, is guilty of an impeachable offense warranting removal from office.

20. Refusal to Comply with Subpoenas

In his conduct of the office of President of the United States, Donald J. Trump, contrary to his oath faithfully to execute the office of President of the United States and, to the best of his ability, preserve, protect, and defend the Constitution of the United States, and in violation of his constitutional duty to take care that the laws be faithfully executed, has failed without lawful cause or excuse to produce witnesses, papers, and things as directed by duly authorized subpoenas issued by the Committee on the Judiciary of the House of Representatives on April 22, 2019, and the Committee on Oversight and Government Reform of the House of Representatives on April 2, 2019. The subpoenaed witnesses, papers, and things were deemed necessary by the Committees in order to resolve by direct evidence fundamental, factual questions relating to Presidential direction, knowledge, or approval of actions demonstrated by other evidence to be potential grounds for impeachment of the President, including matters involving security clearances and "Russiagate."

In refusing to produce these witnesses, papers, and things Donald J. Trump, substituting his judgment as to what materials were necessary for the inquiries, interposed the powers of the Presidency against the lawful subpoenas of the House of Representatives, thereby assuming to himself functions and judgments necessary to the exercise of the sole power of impeachment vested by the Constitution in the House of Representatives. In all of this, Donald J. Trump has acted in a manner contrary to his trust as President and subversive of constitutional government, to the great prejudice of the cause of law and justice, and to the manifest injury of the people of the United States. Wherefore, Donald J.

Trump, by such conduct, warrants impeachment and trial, and removal from office.

21. Declaration of Emergency Without Basis In Order to Violate the Will of Congress

In his conduct while President of the United States, Donald J. Trump, in violation of his constitutional oath to faithfully execute the office of President of the United States and, to the best of his ability, preserve, protect, and defend the Constitution of the United States, and in violation of his constitutional duty under Article II, Section 1 of the Constitution "to take care that the laws be faithfully executed," has declared a state of emergency in the absence of any actual emergency in order to violate the will of Congress and provide deadly weapons to Saudi Arabia for use in its assault on civilians in Yemen.

On May 24, 2019, the Secretary of State announced this policy, justifying it as a means "to deter Iranian aggression." No evidence of Iranian aggression was offered, but President Trump and his subordinates had in the preceding days and weeks been engaged in actions that might provoke Iranian "aggression," including threatening attacks on Iran, moving troops and weapons to the region, declaring part of the Iranian military to be a terrorist organization, producing allegations against Iran widely doubted even by U.S. officials, and -- indeed -- providing weapons to Saudi Arabia.

Congress had been blocking the sale of certain weapons to Saudi Arabia, and the clear purpose of declaring a false emergency was to subvert the will of Congress.

In these actions and decisions, President Donald J. Trump has acted in a manner contrary to his trust as President, and subversive of constitutional government, to the prejudice of the cause of law and justice and to the manifest injury of the people of the United States. Wherefore, President Donald J. Trump, by such conduct, is guilty of an impeachable offense warranting removal from office.

22. Illegal Proliferation of Nuclear Technology

In his conduct while President of the United States, Donald J. Trump, in violation of his constitutional oath to faithfully execute the office of President of the United States and, to the best of his ability, preserve, protect, and defend the Constitution of the United States, and in violation of his constitutional duty under Article II, Section 1 of the Constitution "to take care that the laws be faithfully executed," has sought to illegally transfer nuclear technology to the government of Saudi Arabia.

As documented in the July 2019 report by the House Committee on Oversight and Reform, "Corporate and Foreign Interests Behind White House Push to Transfer U.S. Nuclear Technology to Saudi Arabia," under Section 123 of the Atomic Energy Act, approval of Congress is required to transfer nuclear technology to a foreign country. Congress has not given its approval to such transfers to Saudi Arabia, which has not committed to avoiding activities linked to proliferation, but has, on the contrary, publicly threatened to develop nuclear weapons. President Donald J. Trump has nonetheless made efforts on behalf of those who would profit financially to transfer nuclear technology to Saudi Arabia.

President Donald J. Trump has, moreover, completely refused to cooperate with the Congressional Committee investigation of this matter, and not produced a single document requested.

In these actions and decisions, President Donald J. Trump has acted in a manner contrary to his trust as President, and subversive of constitutional government, to the prejudice of the cause of law and justice and to the manifest injury of the people of the United States and the world. Wherefore, President Donald J. Trump, by such conduct, is guilty of an impeachable offense warranting removal from office.

23. Illegally Removing the United States from the Intermediate-Range Nuclear Forces Treaty

In his conduct while President of the United States, Donald J. Trump, in violation of his constitutional oath to faithfully execute the office of President of the United States and, to the best of his ability, preserve, protect, and defend the Constitution of the United States, and in violation of his constitutional duty under Article II, Section 1 of the Constitution "to take care that the laws be faithfully executed," has illegally removed the United States from the Intermediate-Range Nuclear Forces (INF) Treaty.

The INF Treaty was signed by President Reagan on December 8, 1987, and ratified by consent of the U.S. Senate on May 27, 1988, thereby becoming the supreme law of the land under Article VI, paragraph 2 of the U.S. Constitution. The INF Treaty allows withdrawal only if "extraordinary events related to the subject matter of this Treaty have jeopardized its supreme interests."

The INF Treaty provides for intrusive on-site inspections, backed up by mutual verification by satellite and other monitoring mechanisms, and a Special Verification Commission to resolve any disputes about whether violations have occurred. Whether or not Russian development and deployment of its new 9M729 missile constitutes a "material breach" of the treaty is a matter to be dealt with by the provisions of the treaty itself and cannot satisfy the legal requirement for withdrawal.

By illegally withdrawing from the INF Treaty, President Donald J. Trump has acted in a manner contrary to his trust as President, and subversive of constitutional government, to the prejudice of the cause of law and justice and to the manifest injury of the people of the United States and the world. Wherefore, President Donald J. Trump, by such conduct, is guilty of an impeachable offense warranting removal from office.

24. Seeking to Use Foreign Governments' Resources Against Political Rivals

In his conduct while President of the United States, Donald J. Trump, in violation of his constitutional oath to faithfully execute the office of President of the United States and, to the best of his ability, preserve, protect, and defend the Constitution of the United States, and in violation of his constitutional duty under Article II, Section 1 of the Constitution "to take care that the laws be faithfully executed," has sought to pressure the government of Ukraine to investigate alleged actions of Democratic party rivals including presidential candidate Joseph Biden.

According to the White House summary of a July 25, 2019, phone call between President Trump and Ukrainian President Zelensky, President Trump urged President Zelensky to investigate Joseph Biden as well as other matters related to "Russiagate." As pressure on Zelensky, Trump was withholding funding for weapons that had been appropriated by Congress. Asked about this quid pro quo, acting White House Chief of Staff Mick Mulvaney openly admitted to it.

Asked on camera about urging a foreign government to investigate a political rival, President Trump openly urged Ukraine again to investigate Biden and asked China to do so as well.

Despite this open embrace of his actions, President Trump publicly suggested that whoever had made the content of his call with President Zelensky known should be killed.

In these and similar actions and decisions, President Donald J. Trump has acted in a manner contrary to his trust as President, and subversive of constitutional government, to the prejudice of the cause of law and justice and to the manifest injury of the people of the United States. Wherefore, President Donald J. Trump, by such conduct, is guilty of an impeachable offense warranting removal from office.

25. Refusal to Comply with Impeachment Inquiry

In his conduct while President of the United States, Donald J. Trump, in violation of his constitutional oath to faithfully execute the office of President of the United States and, to the best of his ability, preserve, protect, and defend the Constitution of the United States, and in violation of his constitutional duty under Article II, Section 1 of the Constitution "to take care that the laws be faithfully executed," has refused to comply with subpoenas issued by Congress as part of an inquiry of impeachment.

On July 27, 1974, the House Committee on the Judiciary adopted an article of impeachment against then-President Richard M. Nixon accusing him of failing to comply with Congressional subpoenas. President Donald J. Trump has similarly refused to comply with subpoenas.

Counsel to the President Pat A. Cipollone has written a letter stating that President Trump will not comply with subpoenas related to impeachment investigations. The Defense Department, under President Trump, has stated a similar intent to refuse to comply. Congressional attorneys have acknowledged that President Trump is obstructing the impeachment inquiry. Such obstruction is itself an impeachable offense.

In these ways, President Donald J. Trump has acted in a manner contrary to his trust as President, and subversive of constitutional government, to the prejudice of the cause of law and justice and to the manifest injury of the people of the United States. Wherefore, President Donald J. Trump, by such conduct, is guilty of an impeachable offense warranting removal from office.

Impeachment Strategy

Like many tools, impeachment can be used for better or worse, skillfully or recklessly, wisely or in the manner in which some organizations and wealthy individuals are now pursuing it.

As documented in John Nichols' book *The Genius of Impeachment*, the U.S. Congress has used impeachment a great many times, against presidents and many other officials, often creating effective pressure for reform prior to actually impeaching. It's a process that has sometimes taken months, other times years. But the U.S. government would be even less representative than it is of the public will without this history.

Moves to impeach presidents, including Truman and Nixon, did a world of good. Popular, and not strictly partisan, movements advanced principled demands around substantive abuses of power. While the worst war crimes were not passed as articles of impeachment, they were part of the discussion.

The results included, not just the end of particular abuses, but the creation of a climate in which others expected to be held accountable.

The impeachment of Bill Clinton, in contrast, focused with such hypocrisy, partisanship, and vindictiveness on such a lesser charge -- with serious offenses, never entering the discussion -- that the result was not only no conviction in the Senate and no reform in the government, but also a horribly damaging aversion to the tool of impeachment.

The refusal of Congress to meet the public demand for the impeachment of George W. Bush cemented in place a sense of presidential impunity – especially on war powers – that has been flaunted by Bush, Obama, and now Donald Trump. This has helped to transfer powers from Congress to the White House, and Congress members' diminishing identification with their branch of government (together with the increase in "campaign contributions") has radically increased their identification with their political parties. This process erodes representative government. It must be undone. But it must be undone in a manner that does not make things even worse.

Since inauguration day 2017, RootsAction.org has been building a list of proper impeachable offenses. These are major abuses of power that set horrific precedents, and they are documented beyond any reasonable dispute. They require no investigation, only political will. Impeachment and removal on these grounds, if created by public demand, would create wonderful precedents, including the threat of a similar impeachment hanging over the head of Mike Pence or whoever next enters the oval office. Allowing these abuses to go unchecked, in contrast, risks nuclear and environmental apocalypse and guarantees severe suffering for millions. It also guarantees that the office of the presidency will be a tyrannical institution, no matter the merits of the man or woman who enters into it.

Nowhere to be found on this list of impeachable offenses: Russia.

Others are advocating Trump's impeachment because of what they call a Russian "act of war" against the United States, feeding right into the Trump administration's own new policies of declaring cyber- and other crimes to be acts of war to be responded to with actual war. This type of impeachment campaign risks getting us all killed. It also risks a failure to convict due to lack of evidence -- which failure would truly entrench dictatorial powers beyond any likely reform.

"Russiagate" was begun as a distraction from the content of Democratic Party emails, which documented unfair treatment of candidate Bernie Sanders by the party establishment. The claim that the Russian government or Trump was behind leaking those emails has yet to be proven. But if it were proven, it would be one more outrage to pile onto a list that includes the mistreatment of Sanders that the emails confirmed. Other serious outrages involving "assaults on our democracy":

- The massive boost that corporate media,

especially cable news, chose to give to Donald Trump in 2015 and 2016.

- The intimidation and incitement to violence engaged in by candidate Trump.
- The racist removal of voters from the roles by Republican governors and legislatures.
- The unverifiable vote counting, and the failure to do proper counts even where possible.
- The denial of a popular outcome by the Electoral College.
- The exclusion of most candidates from the media and the nationally-televised debates.
- The gargantuan financial corruption by corporate interests.
- The hurdles placed in the way of registering to vote.
- The ID laws and other hurdles placed in the way of voting.

This was not an election system that could be noticeably worsened or improved by a single act of leaking, no matter how inappropriate the source.

Nor have we yet seen evidence that would hold up in a court or in the U.S. Senate to prove that the Russian government organized any serious campaign on social media that could effect the election, much less that it did so together with Trump. That Russian state media outlets openly tended to prefer Trump to Clinton had no major impact on the election, involved Trump in no impeachable offense, and parallels the sorts of positions that U.S. state and private media outlets routinely take in elections around the world.

That the United States government has in recent decades taken more serious steps to interfere in 84 elections including in Russia, and actually overthrown 36 governments, attempted to assassinate over 50 foreign leaders, and bombed over 30 countries (see davidswanson.org/warlist), does not in any way excuse similar crimes by others. But it illuminates the hypocrisy of many who want Trump impeached over "Russia's assault on our democracy."

Let's build a wise, effective, strategic movement for impeachment, not for World War III.

Impeachment FAQ

But we don't want Mike Pence to become president, do we?

The question of who is worse, the current president or the vice president, is a very different question from this one: "Who is worse, President Trump in an era of unchecked power and immunity, or President Pence in an age of popular sovereignty with the threat of impeachment looming behind every high-crime-and-misdemeanor that comes up for consideration by the White House?" We believe changing the office of the presidency into one that can be lost for substantive crimes and abuses — a radical change from its current state — would be a crucial step toward genuine democracy. Part of that significance would derive from the benefits of building the movement that imposes impeachment on a corrupted and partisan and reluctant Congress. Deep and long-term political change comes principally from movement-building, which is what will prevent future Trumps and Pences. As

Trump's reign of disaster continues, justifications for allowing it to continue appear ever weaker. And, if the most sycophantic worshiper of Trump on the national stage, Mike Pence, becomes president after the removal of a discredited Trump, Pence will be one of the weakest presidents in modern history. Even weaker than Gerald Ford, who had far more distance from Nixon, the discredited president he replaced. In addition, one of our draft articles of impeachment applies to both Trump and Pence.

Why punish a successful businessman?

We can set aside the legality and morality of Trump's business success, and the question of how successful he has been. A campaign to impeach him for his violations of the Constitution's emoluments clauses can hold the position that Trump is perfectly welcome to keep all of his businesses and loans. He just cannot simultaneously hold an office in which they create gross violations of the U.S. Constitution. Past presidents have sold off their assets or placed them in a blind trust. A blind trust would not, however, be blind for Trump who would inevitably learn of the approval of new towers or the sale of properties. Selling (and using a truly blind trust to do so) was Trump's only option other than not being president. He chose not to take his only constitutional choice.

Is this partisanship?

A great many people do anything political for partisan reasons. It is inevitable that people will favor or oppose impeaching Trump for partisan reasons. But they need not. The charges against Trump are largely unprecedented. They should apply to him and any future presidents who engage in similar abuses, regardless of party. Someone who voted for Trump as a way out of corruption should want him impeached as much as someone who voted against him for the same reason. Trump is now the worst possible "insider" — using public office for personal greed.

Is this personal?

A great many people focus their political interest on personalities rather than policies. They forbid themselves to praise a good action by a politician who mostly makes bad ones, or to condemn a bad one by a hero. They make heroes of whoever is not their enemy, and vice versa. They place greater importance on whether they'd like to be friends with someone than on whether that person will benefit or harm the world. Many will support or oppose impeaching Trump based on whether they consider him awful or inspiring. They shouldn't and need not.

Why not impeach Trump for being a Russian agent?

If such evidence ever emerges, then at that time it should be pursued.

Do you really think Congress will impeach a president?

Yes, it certainly might, especially as the evidence of "high crimes and misdemeanors" accumulates and Trump's popularity sinks even lower than the record lows it has reached — an effect that just opening an impeachment process has usually contributed to. But even an unsuccessful impeachment effort can have seriously beneficial results, including helping to end the Vietnam War and ending Nixon's presidency.

Isn't it pointless and counterproductive to impeach when the Senate will not convict?

No. First of all, impeachment hearings on serious indisputable public offenses are educational for the public and the media and the Senate. Second, they serve to check a president whose egregious abuses of power have been increasing in light of his apparent impunity and whose recklessness risks environmental and nuclear apocalypse. Third, wise predictions of what the Senate will do can reverse themselves rapidly, as just prior to Nixon's resignation. Fourth, it is the job of the House to comply with the Constitution, and predictions of what the Senate might do cannot excuse a dereliction of duty. Fifth, if there is no impeachment, Trump will claim that he did nothing wrong, and Senators will claim that they never had a chance to consider the matter. Sixth, if there is an impeachment and the Senate does fail to do its job, Senate leadership and individual Senators can be held accountable, including at election time. Isn't identifying and removing lawless Senators worthwhile?

Do you really think everything is normal and nothing radical is needed?

Useful strategies are desperately needed, and impeachment is one of them. Others are marches, sit-ins, petitions, media production, legislation, strikes, refusals to cooperate with illegal actions, protection of those in danger, peace initiatives, local and global moves toward sustainable economies, boycotts, divestments, foreign exchanges, art work, parades, etc., etc. But a nonviolent movement seeking to overturn an abusive government would fantasize about an impeachment provision if it didn't exist. It's one of the best gifts that the drafters of the Constitution gave us. Continuing to neglect the power of impeachment would be a terrible waste.

Isn't impeachment a trick by the evil System which is rotten to the core and wants us to think it is capable of reform?

No. The system may be rotten to the core, but the question is how to fix it. Impeachment can be a very useful tool for that, and is clearly not one longed for by either big political party.

Do you really think something as radical as impeachment is needed?

If it's not needed now, when would it be?

Shouldn't we all focus on electing Democrats to Congress first?

No. Numerous impeachment efforts over the centuries, of presidents and many other high officials, have led to reforms and resignations short of reaching impeachments or convictions. In numerous cases, representatives and senators have put justice ahead of partisanship. In numerous cases, the effort has had to build for months or years before having an impact. In numerous cases, whether impeachment efforts or all sorts of other dramatic social and political changes, the common wisdom has predicted defeat until shortly prior to victory. It is also important for us to understand the position of the leaders of the Democratic Party, based on their past performance and their public statements. They apparently do not want a Trump impeachment, not now or ever. If we are going to make impeachment happen, if we are going to move members of either party to support it, and if we are going to make it effective in achieving reform and setting a precedent, then we need to advance impeachment as a non-partisan and urgent matter. It's urgency is no pretense. Every moment he remains in office, Trump increases the risk of environmental and/or nuclear catastrophe.

Wasn't impeaching Clinton a bad idea, thus making all impeachments bad ideas?

The impeachment of Bill Clinton was not driven by public demand, and was, in fact, unpopular with the U.S. public. Other impeachments have been very popular with the public. Clinton had 66% approval, while Trump has consistently been somewhere around 40%. Clinton was impeached for how he responded to an investigation that turned up very little. Trump could be impeached in a very similar manner, or he could be impeached for any number of important and indisputable abuses of power. And those abuses could be made known to the U.S. public through impeachment hearings of the sort that had a powerful impact on the public during the process to impeach Richard Nixon. While impeaching Clinton was unpopular, it did not negatively impact Republicans in any major way; they kept control of both houses of Congress and claimed the White House.

If this succeeds, then who will be President?

If Donald Trump is impeached, convicted, and removed from office, Vice President Mike Pence will become President until January 2021. If Mike Pence is impeached and convicted and removed from office (or resigns) prior to Trump being removed from office, then Pence's replacement (nominated by Trump and confirmed by Congress) will become President – which is how Gerald Ford became president. If Pence is impeached and removed from office after becoming President, then, similarly, whoever replaced him as Vice President will replace him as President until January 2021. If by some incredible (not to say impossible) combination of events both President Trump and Vice President Pence are simultaneously removed from office, House Speaker Nancy Pelosi will become President, and she will nominate a Vice President who will require Congressional confirmation. The important answer is that whoever becomes President after an impeachment and conviction will know that stepping out of line and abusing power can result in his or her removal. His or her term will end in January 2021 unless he or she is elected to four more years -- as Gerald Ford was not.

About RootsAction.org

RootsAction is an online initiative dedicated to galvanizing people who are committed to economic fairness, equal rights for all, civil liberties, environmental protection -- and defunding endless wars.

We will not be silent as President Trump and Congress continue to squander billions of dollars on foreign wars, causing destruction and hatred overseas while failing to meet the needs of the vast majority of people in our country.

We will not stand by as people lose their jobs, homes, healthcare and income due to corporatist policies abetted by both major parties.

We will take action -- independent of both party leaderships.

That's why RootsAction has been strongly endorsed by such respected, independent-minded progressives as Jim Hightower, Barbara Ehrenreich, Cornel West, Daniel Ellsberg, Glenn Greenwald, Naomi Klein, Bill Fletcher Jr., Laura Flanders, former U.S. Senator James Abourezk, Frances Fox Piven, Lila Garrett, Phil Donahue, Sonali Kolhatkar, and many others.

When progressives have fallen into making excuses for an unjust and untenable status quo -- they've helped corporate-allied "populists" of the right wing to masquerade as the agents of change.

RootsAction is mobilizing behind policies that actually address the immense economic, social, racial and environmental problems facing our country. The goal is to organize people who are already active into an independent political force, while reaching out in a genuinely populist voice to those who are not committed progressives. This is crucial for defeating the corporate-financed and media-fueled right wing, which so deftly utilizes racism, fear, myth and outright lies.

RootsAction pledges to resist the policies of the

Republican regime at every turn, while confronting the Democratic Party's tendency to give ground to extremist proposals in the name of "bipartisanship."

One of the most heartening recent developments in our country is the rise of independent media that reach millions each day with reporting that exposes not just threats from the extreme right, but also vacillation and corruption among Democrats. These millions represent a base of informed, active Americans that RootsAction seeks to empower and mobilize.

Corporate power over both major parties is afflicting and poisoning the body politic. Genuine democracy is the antidote.

RootsAction is open to all those who seek a more just and peaceful world; contact us with your ideas for issues we should address and actions we should take.

RootsAction.org
1500 West El Camino Ave #370
Sacramento, CA 95833
USA

www.ingramcontent.com/pod-product-compliance
Lightning Source LLC
Chambersburg PA
CBHW060346050426
42336CB00050B/2147